THE MINDFULNESS
JOURNAL FOR TEENS

the MINDFULNESS JOURNAL for TEENS

Prompts and Practices to Help You Stay Cool, Calm, and Present

Jennie Marie Battistin, MA, LMFT

ROCKRIDGE
PRESS

For general information on our other products and services or to obtain technical support, please contact our Customer Care Department within the United States at (866) 744-2665, or outside the United States at (510) 253-0500.

Rockridge Press publishes its books in a variety of electronic and print formats. Some content that appears in print may not be available in electronic books, and vice versa.

TRADEMARKS: Rockridge Press and the Rockridge Press logo are trademarks or registered trademarks of Callisto Media Inc. and/or its affiliates, in the United States and other countries, and may not be used without written permission. All other trademarks are the property of their respective owners. Rockridge Press is not associated with any product or vendor mentioned in this book.

Interior Designer: Angela Navarra

Cover Designer: Sean Doyle

Art Producer: Sara Feinstein

Editor: Lauren O'Neal

Production Editor: Andrew Yackira

All illustrations used under license from iStock.com. Author photo courtesy of © Tim Sabatino with Theta Creata Studios.

ISBN: Print 978-1-64611-283-8

R0

TABLE OF CONTENTS

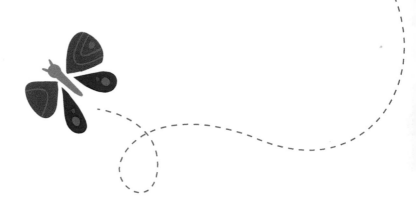

LEARNING TO LIVE IN THE
PRESENT MOMENT
IS PART OF THE PATH OF JOY.

—Sarah Ban Breathnach

THIS JOURNAL BELONGS TO:

INTRODUCTION

Welcome to mindfulness through journaling! Whether you're new to mindfulness or not, journaling is an amazing way to more deeply connect with mindfulness concepts.

Having worked with thousands of teenagers—and raised five of my own—I've seen firsthand the tremendous benefits of mindfulness for teens. You can start to see these benefits with just 5 to 10 minutes of practice a day. Many of my clients say they enjoy the benefits of mindfulness so much that they often spend 30 minutes or more on mindfulness-based exercises, techniques, and meditations every day.

What Does "Mindfulness" Mean?

How many times have you caught your mind aimlessly wandering when you should be concentrating on homework, classwork, or some other task? When your mind takes flight, you lose touch with the present and, without realizing it, become preoccupied—maybe with thoughts about something that happened in the past, worries about the future, or frustrations about some other issue.

Mindfulness is being fully present in the moment. It means you're aware of what you're doing, how you're feeling, and where you are, without being overwhelmed by what's happening around you. No matter how far away your thoughts drift, mindfulness can bring you back to the present and encourage you to focus on the task at hand, your current emotions, and your present thoughts. It's more than just sitting silently in a quiet place. It unleashes your mind's natural curiosity and helps you approach everything with acceptance and compassion for yourself and others.

We're all born with the ability to be mindful, but we can get better at it by using various techniques, exercises, and activities like sports or yoga. It's best to focus on the practice itself rather than the benefits—but there are powerful benefits. Being mindful can help reduce stress levels, improve focus, boost academic performance, amplify strengths, improve weaknesses, build awareness, increase insight, and enhance overall well-being.

It's important to understand that this journal doesn't replace professional therapeutic guidance. If you're experiencing deeper issues, mental health struggles, or difficult family or friend relationships, I encourage you to seek out a licensed therapist.

How to Use This Journal

This journal is designed to be a practical, easy, and fun tool for living mindfully. It's a creative and interactive space for learning mindfulness with a sense of joy—so break out your markers and colored pencils if you want! This book contains a series of writing prompts and reflections, meditations, exercises, and inspirational quotes to help you incorporate mindfulness into your daily life. Commit to one or two exercises or prompts every day—this will help mindfulness become part of your daily life.

While you'll probably start to see some benefits from this journaling process within 30 days, mindfulness is not a 30-day challenge fad. It's a lifetime habit that you can use to make *everything* better. It's important to stick to it, even if you struggle at first. Once you get into your mindfulness groove, it can start to become second nature within a couple of weeks. You're setting foot on the path of lifelong mindfulness. Enjoy the journey!

HERE AND NOW

When did you last spend time with your thoughts, grounded in the here and now? In the hustle and bustle of everyday life, it's easy to forget to be with your mind in the present moment. You can get caught up dwelling on the past or considering the what-ifs of the future. But just 5 to 10 minutes of daily mindfulness can help you reel in your wandering mind and bring you mental peace, clarity, and a better understanding of yourself and your surroundings. The prompts and practices in this section will help you tune into yourself and live in the moment.

Pause. Consider the here and now, this very moment. Notice your breath, any sensations in your body, and any feelings that come up. Journal about engaging with mindfulness. Are you nervous? Uncertain? Hopeful? Excited?

....

....

....

....

....

....

....

....

....

Do you ever carry yesterday's worries into today? What worry are you holding on to right now? Consider what it would be like to let go of those worries. Journal your thoughts.

Just Breathe

An important part of being mindful is accepting this moment. Paying attention to our breath can help us do that. Try both of the breathing techniques described below.

5-7-8 Breathing

- Find a comfortable place to sit, and place your hands over your belly button.

- Breathe in through your nose for a count of 5.

- Hold your breath for a count of 7.

- Breathe out through your mouth, forcefully, for a count of 8.

- Repeat three times.

4-Square Breathing

- Find a comfortable place to sit, and place your hands over your belly button.

- Breathe in through your nose for a count of 4.

- Hold your breath for a count of 4.

- Breathe out through your mouth for a count of 4.

- Hold your breath for a count of 4.

- Repeat four times.

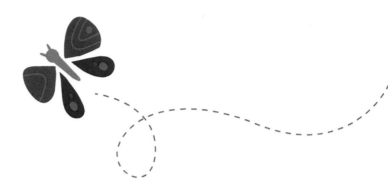

WHAT WOULD IT BE LIKE IF I COULD ACCEPT LIFE— ACCEPT THIS MOMENT— EXACTLY AS IT IS?

—Tara Brach

Sometimes our thoughts can wander without direction or purpose. This can lead to being distracted. Without judgment, notice what thoughts have been wandering through your mind today. Write them down.

....

....

....

....

....

....

....

....

....

....

Step by Step

Here is a positive way to help mindfully consider problems and find solutions.

Step 1: Identify the Problem

Consider a problem you're facing. Write down your problem as clearly as possible. Ask yourself questions like: What is the problem? How have I responded so far? What result was/am I expecting?

....

....

....

....

....

....

Step 2: Outline Your Solutions

The key to solving your problem is to find realistic solutions. Write down the ideal solution first, and then think outside the box. Think of at least three solutions total.

Step 3: List Your Strategies

For each solution, write down at least three strategies or steps for making the solution happen.

....

....

....

....

....

....

....

....

....

Step 4: Open Yourself to Possibilities

Take a moment to evaluate each strategy. List the pros and cons. Now pick the best strategy to solve the problem.

....

....

....

....

....

....

....

....

....

Step 5: Getting Results

Now that you have your best strategy in place, it's time to get results. Write down a step-by-step process of how you will implement the strategy to solve the problem. That's it!

....

....

....

....

....

....

....

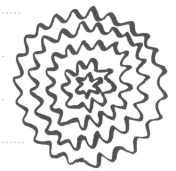

....

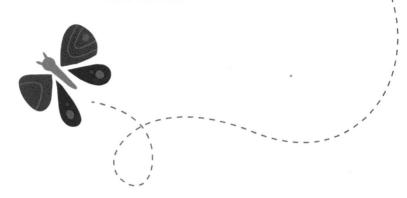

LIVE THE ACTUAL MOMENT. ONLY THIS ACTUAL MOMENT IS LIFE.

—Thích Nhất Hạnh

Have you heard the phrase "Learn from your mistakes"? Journal about how you cope with mistakes and failure and what you have learned from your mistakes. After journaling, say out loud to yourself, "I learn from my mistakes."

....

....

....

....

....

....

....

....

....

Do you ever stop to take in the space around you?
Does it affect you in any particular way? What feelings
or sensations do you notice as you observe it?

....

....

....

....

....

....

....

....

....

....

Tall and Proud

Your posture can affect how you approach your day. Taking a moment to address the day tall and proud can have a positive influence. Try the technique of "power posing" to start your day.

- Stand in front of a mirror with your feet shoulder-width apart and your hands on your hips.

- Look at yourself in the eyes while taking five deep breaths.

- Say out loud or to yourself, "I seek strength, intelligence, and courage."

- Stand for one minute in this pose, looking at yourself and holding these words to be true.

- Say out loud or to yourself, "I find strength, intelligence, and courage."

- Look at yourself and hold these words to be true.

- Say out loud or to yourself, "I have strength, intelligence, and courage."

- Look at yourself and hold these words to be true.

- Say out loud or to yourself, "I am strong, intelligent, and courageous."

- Look at yourself and hold those words to be true.

- Now close your eyes and imagine yourself taking care of all the tasks of the day and feeling proud.

- To finish, take four deep, slow breaths.

When you spend time with a close friend, what positive attributes do they demonstrate or bring out in you? Notice any feelings that arise as you consider your friendships. Write about your thoughts.

....

....

....

....

....

....

....

....

....

....

Taking a moment to be grateful can create a positive mind-set and help us handle the ups and downs of each day. Draw a picture of a garden. In your garden, instead of flowers or vegetables, write out positive words of gratitude sprouting from the ground.

Something Sweet

Most of us aren't mindful when eating, often doing something else at the same time, such as watching TV or looking at social media. Mindful eating is a practical way to add mindfulness to your day. Try this delicious mindfulness exercise with a piece of candy.

- Take a moment to notice the wrapper around the candy. Does the light catch on the wrapper? What color is it?

- Bring the candy up to your nose. Can you smell the candy through the wrapper? Notice any sensations in your nose and mouth as you smell the candy.

- Close your eyes and roll the candy around in your hand. What does it feel like? Is it hard or soft?

- Unwrap the candy. Notice any sensations as you unwrap the candy.

- Smell the candy without the wrapper and notice any sensations.

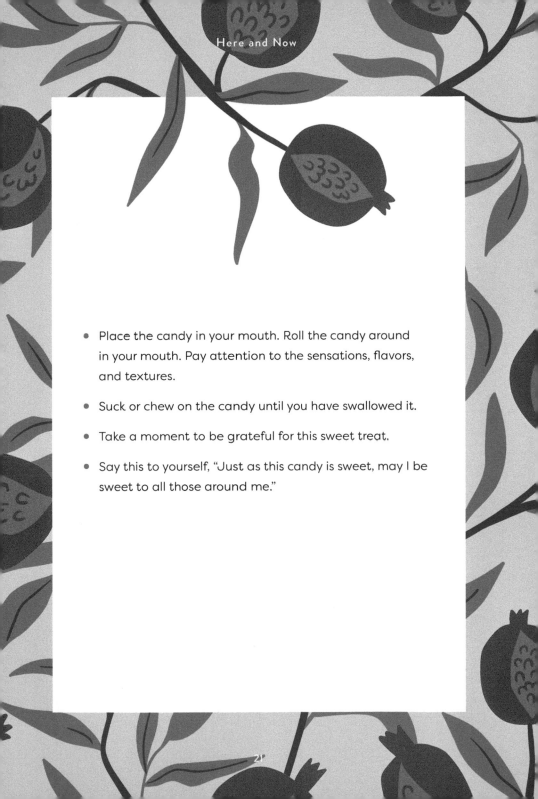

- Place the candy in your mouth. Roll the candy around in your mouth. Pay attention to the sensations, flavors, and textures.

- Suck or chew on the candy until you have swallowed it.

- Take a moment to be grateful for this sweet treat.

- Say this to yourself, "Just as this candy is sweet, may I be sweet to all those around me."

Self-care is purposefully doing something to help your physical, emotional, and/or mental health, like reading a good book, taking a nap, or eating healthy foods. What are your thoughts on this concept? What is a self-care activity you can do today?

....

....

....

....

....

....

....

....

....

It's natural to embrace the good things in life, but what would it be like to accept the bad and ugly moments too? Take a minute to sit with some of the less-than-ideal events of the past few days. Say to yourself, "It's okay to feel bad or experience an ugly moment. This will pass." Journal your thoughts. Consider drawing a butterfly over your words to represent that these feelings won't last forever.

Body Scan

A "body-scan meditation" can increase awareness of the body, helping you focus and be less reactive. For this exercise, consider recording yourself reading the script and playing it back, or finding a body-scan meditation on YouTube or the Calm app.

- Find a comfortable place to lie down.

- Notice your toes. Notice how they feel right now. Notice each toe.

- Notice your right foot. Notice your left foot. Notice the temperature of your feet—cold, warm, or hot.

- Notice your ankles. Take a moment to feel your ankles.

- Now scan up and down your left and right leg from ankle to hip. Notice any sensations you feel. Stop at your knees. Notice your knees.

- Focus your attention on your back. Notice any sensations. Scan up and down your back.

- Move your focus from your back around your sides to your belly. Notice any sensations around your belly.

- Mentally scan up and down from your belly to your neck.

- Now notice your shoulders. Scan across from shoulder to shoulder, noticing any sensations.

- Now scan from your right shoulder to your right hand. Notice each finger on your right hand. Notice how your fingers feel. Scan across the palm of your hand to your wrist. Scan up your arm to your elbow. Notice any sensations in your elbow.

- Now scan up your right arm back to your shoulder. Scan from your right shoulder to your left shoulder. Scan your left arm and hand the same way you scanned your right arm and hand.

- When you get to the top of your left shoulder again, scan up to your neck. Notice any sensations in your neck.

- Now turn your attention to your face and head. Scan across your chin, lips, nose, eyes, ears, forehead, and head.

- Staying in passive observation, scan your body as a whole. Become fully aware of each part of your body. If you notice any sensation of interest, you can linger for a moment on those sensations. Scan up and down your body twice.

- Now take three deep, energizing breaths. Breathe in deeply and exhale deeply. Become fully alert and energetic.

One way to stay grounded in today is to consider what today has to offer. Write down something you're thankful for today.

....

....

....

....

....

....

....

....

....

....

Do you rule your mind, or does your mind rule you?
Stop right now. What were your thoughts 10 minutes
ago? What are you feeling toward those thoughts?
Were those feelings or thoughts affecting your
behavior without your awareness?

....

....

....

....

....

....

....

....

....

Walk This Way

One way to stay connected in the present is to practice mindful walking.

- Take a walk in the park, in your yard, or on your block.

- Take a moment to notice as each foot makes contact with the ground and as it lifts to take another step.

- Notice where your arms are as you walk.

- If your thoughts begin to wander, it's okay. Gently coach your focus back to your walking. Say to yourself, "Pay attention; stay present."

- Take a deep breath. Do you notice any smells? Are the smells pleasant or unpleasant?

- Now take a moment to observe the area around you. Are there trees, plants, or flowers? Any animals or birds? People? Buildings?

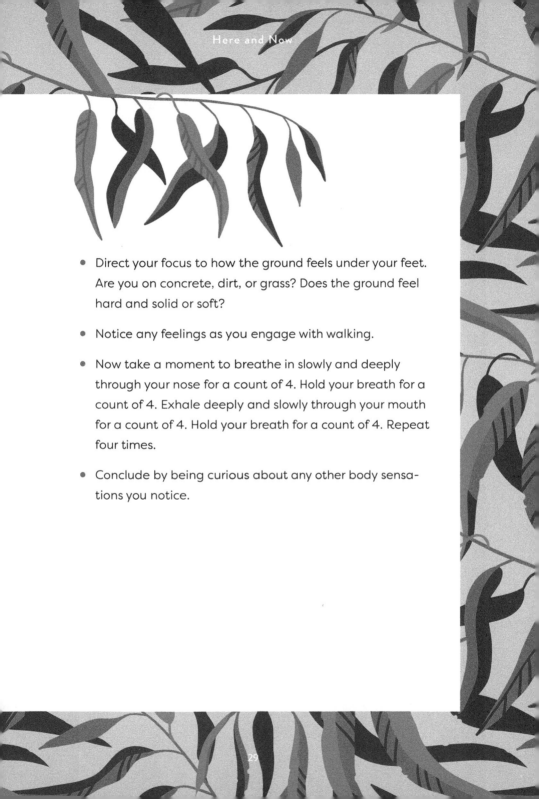

- Direct your focus to how the ground feels under your feet. Are you on concrete, dirt, or grass? Does the ground feel hard and solid or soft?

- Notice any feelings as you engage with walking.

- Now take a moment to breathe in slowly and deeply through your nose for a count of 4. Hold your breath for a count of 4. Exhale deeply and slowly through your mouth for a count of 4. Hold your breath for a count of 4. Repeat four times.

- Conclude by being curious about any other body sensations you notice.

Consider the mundane tasks you do each day—brushing your teeth, walking or driving to school, showering—and practice being mindful and focused on those tasks. Make a list of mundane tasks and pick one to practice engaging with mindfully this week.

Self-awareness is the ability to understand and be consciously aware of your body, feelings, and thoughts. It can help you make better decisions, maximize your strengths, and improve your weaknesses. For example, if you're tapping your foot during a test, self-awareness might tell you that you're nervous. Self-awareness can be a fence to the wandering mind. List the strengths and weaknesses you'd like to be aware of in the coming week.

Strengths

Weaknesses

How are you feeling about your mindfulness journey so far? Are you starting to get into a groove? What are you enjoying? Any challenges with mindfulness?

....

....

....

....

....

....

....

....

....

....

Set a timer for five minutes. Imagine your thoughts have a volume control like a radio. Turn the volume down on your thoughts. Imagine the night sky and stay focused on the limitlessness beyond Earth's atmosphere. Try to clear your mind of thoughts. Notice your breath as you stare into the endless night sky. After the five minutes are over, write down any thoughts or feelings that popped up.

Rather than labeling feelings "good" or "bad," try thinking of them as either "pleasant" or "unpleasant." Pleasant feelings might be joy, hope, happiness, contentment, gratitude, confidence, and so on. What pleasant feeling would you like to invite into your day? Write about your thoughts, ending by actively inviting that feeling into your day.

....

....

....

....

....

....

....

I invite .... into my day.

Shift Key

Are you feeling any unpleasant feelings today? Feelings can go up and down like a roller coaster sometimes. One way to manage unpleasant feelings is to actively engage and shift the feelings toward more pleasant feelings. Give this exercise a try.

- Find a comfortable place to sit or lie down.

- Take three slow, deep breaths.

- Close your eyes.

- Notice any unpleasant feelings.

- Scan your body and notice where the emotion is located. Place your hands over that area.

- Smile and say out loud or to yourself, "I choose joy." Repeat the phrase three times.

- Smile and say out loud or to yourself, "I choose happiness." Repeat the phrase three times.

- Smile and say out loud or to yourself, "I choose gratitude." Repeat the phrase three times.

- Smile and say out loud or to yourself, "I choose confidence." Repeat the phrase three times.

- Smile and say out loud or to yourself, "I choose self-love." Repeat the phrase three times.

- Smile and open your eyes. Notice the shift in your emotions.

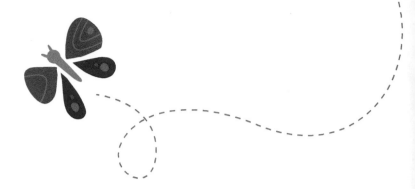

THE BEST WAY TO GET SOMEWHERE IS TO LET GO OF TRYING TO GET ANYWHERE AT ALL.

—Jon Kabat-Zinn

Look around you. Notice what you see, hear, and smell. Reach out and touch something in this space. Notice the feelings you have about staying right here, right now. If there are unpleasant thoughts or feelings, say to yourself, "It's okay. This won't last forever." Write about your experience.

Take a moment to listen to how you're feeling. Are you judging or accepting your feelings? Write down your feelings and your outlook for today.

THE STORY
I TELL MYSELF

We all tell ourselves stories about the events in our lives. Often those stories have more to do with our thoughts than with reality. You might tell yourself something like, "I got a bad grade on that test because I'm not smart enough," when in reality you may not have spent enough time studying, or the test was just really hard. Sometimes it's easy to lose track of how your inner thoughts and narratives play out in your day-to-day life, either positively or negatively. When you change your internal monologues, you can change how you handle situations and live your life.

Your internal voice or narrative can impact your responses to events and people. A person with the internal narrative "I'm not a morning person" might be more irritable on days they have to get up earlier. What do your internal narratives tell you about yourself? Journal your thoughts.

Think about a song that makes you happy. Hum the song to yourself or play it on your phone. Are there specific lines in the song that speak to you most? Write down the lyrics and why they make you happy.

....

....

....

....

....

....

....

....

....

....

Sometimes you need to take a moment and do something nice for yourself. For example, if you overcame a challenge, pat yourself on the back and say, "Hey, that was tough, but I did well." How have you taken care of yourself lately? How can you be nice to yourself today?

....

....

....

....

....

....

....

....

....

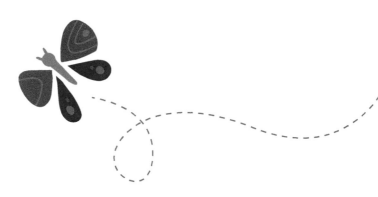

YOU'RE GOING TO TELL YOURSELF STORIES ANYWAY, SO WHY NOT **TELL YOURSELF** THE GOOD ONES?

—Jodie Rogers

Does doubt ever hold you back? Do you believe in yourself? Journal your thoughts.

What stories have you told yourself that have created fears? What would happen if you were curious about fear? What fear has stopped you in the past? What would you pursue if fear didn't stop you?

....

....

....

....

....

....

....

....

....

Mindcraft

Have you ever played the video game *Minecraft*? In the world of *Minecraft*, you can build whatever you want. Similarly, your mind can build quite a story. Today, practice your own game called *Mindcraft*. Think about your mind as often as possible. Keep drawing your attention to your mind. This will help build awareness of your mind and the stories you may unknowingly try to create. This may seem simple or silly. It is not. I challenge you to try to draw your attention to your mind at least every 30 minutes.

Do you ever let responsibilities take away any of the fun in life? What would it be like to reclaim the moments of childlike fun in your day?

Do your worries stop you from living in the moment? Do they define how you see yourself at times? What if you could let go of those worries? What would you be doing differently in your life?

Take a moment to reflect on your mindfulness journey so far. What are you learning about yourself? Make a list of things you've learned. Put a plus sign by anything you want to do more of in the coming weeks and a minus sign by anything you want to do less. For anything you'd like to do less, think of how you could shift the thoughts, feelings, or behaviors.

Do you remember a time you had to show courage? Do you consider yourself courageous? Notice any sensation you feel in your body as you consider this question. Say to yourself, "I am courageous, bold, and unstoppable." Write your thoughts.

....

....

....

....

....

....

....

....

....

Remember the Cowardly Lion from *The Wizard of Oz*? In the end, he turned out to be a pretty brave beast. Draw a picture that represents your brave beast. In the last exercise, I had you consider the affirmation "I am courageous, bold, and unstoppable." Around the picture, write a similar positive affirmation that you can use to be mindful of your courage.

Meditation Medicine

Consider meditation your medicine for healing, letting go of critical stories about yourself, and accepting yourself exactly as you are. Try this mediation to increase your self-acceptance.

- Find a comfortable place to sit or lie down.

- Place your hands over your belly button.

- Slowly inhale for a count of 4. Hold your breath for a count of 4. Slowly exhale for a count of 4. Hold your breath for a count of 4. Repeat four times.

- Take a moment to celebrate your life story. Say out loud four positive thoughts or characteristics that define who you are today. For example, "I have studied well and do my best," "I am upbeat and friendly," "I am caring," "I am a good listener."

- Say out loud, "May I have happiness and joy. May I love and be loved. May I live with peace. May I accept and live life fully." Repeat four times.

- Say out loud, "May I share happiness and joy with others. May I love and share love with others. May others experience peace." Repeat four times.

- Slowly inhale for a count of 4. Hold your breath for a count of 4. Slowly exhale for a count of 4. Hold your breath for a count of 4. Repeat four times.

What are the stories you tell yourself about anxiety?
Do you hold anxious thoughts to be absolute truths?
Do you allow the anxiety to be a story about you?

....

....

....

....

....

....

....

....

....

....

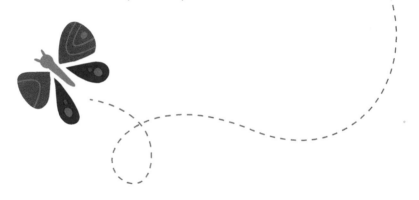

THE STORIES WE TELL OURSELVES ARE THE STORIES THAT DEFINE THE POTENTIALITIES OF OUR EXISTENCE.

—Shekhar Kapur

Looking back, how many times have you worried about what-if scenarios that never materialized? What are five worries you have today? Write them down, then say to yourself, "I am capable and calm. I can handle any possibilities that arise."

....

....

....

....

....

....

....

....

....

Think of the last song that got stuck in your head. Is the song happy, sad, contemplative? What feelings did the song bring up?

....

....

....

....

....

....

....

....

....

....

Take a moment to think about your talents and successes. What are you good at? Write your thoughts.
I am good at . . .

....

....

....

....

....

....

....

....

....

Wind Whisperer

Whatever unpleasant thoughts or feelings you might have today, try not to let them overwhelm you and be your story for the day. Try this exercise: Imagine you open the door to your house and a gust of wind calls to your anxious or sad thoughts. Begin to notice your breath. Each time you exhale, imagine that you're blowing the anxious thoughts or sad feelings out the door to the wind. Imagine the wind taking them away. As you inhale deeply, imagine that the wind pushes happiness and joy your way and you breathe these feelings in. Notice the sensations of your body as you replace the unpleasant thoughts and feelings with pleasant ones.

Do you struggle with insecurities about self-image? What story do you tell yourself when you look in the mirror? Do you notice any feelings of judgment? Any feelings of self-acceptance?

....

....

....

....

....

....

....

....

....

....

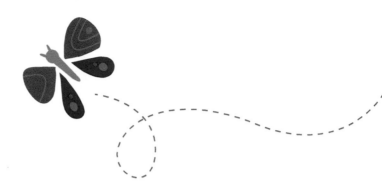

I BELIEVE THAT TELLING OUR STORIES, FIRST TO OURSELVES AND THEN TO ONE ANOTHER AND THE WORLD, IS A REVOLUTIONARY ACT.

—Janet Mock

No one is perfect, but do you feel safe and worthy in your own skin? Are you enough? Do you accept yourself? What does self-acceptance mean to you?

....

....

....

....

....

....

....

....

....

....

Update Your Story

Scrolling through social media can crush your ability to concentrate. It's easy to lose focus of your own story and be carried away in other people's stories. You can start to feel like everyone else has better experiences than you do. Just for today, take a social media vacation and focus on your life story.

- Start your day by saying out loud, "Today I choose my life story."

- Commit to staying away from social media today—no scrolling, no posting.

- Notice any feelings or physical sensations as you make this commitment.

- Consider what you appreciate about your life.

- Say out loud four things that you're grateful for today.

- Take a moment to consider what four tasks you would like to define your day.

- Invite focus into your day to accomplish these tasks.

- Take four deep, slow breaths.

- Say out loud, "I am the designer of my life story. My story is important to me."

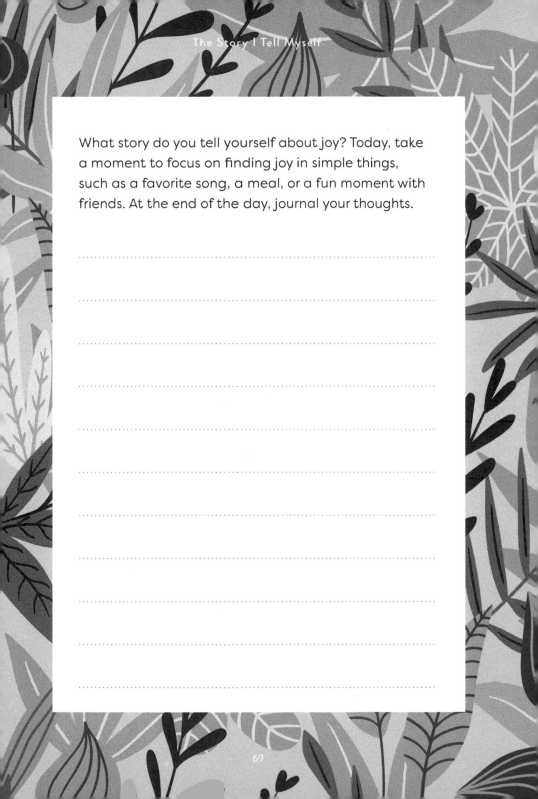

What story do you tell yourself about joy? Today, take a moment to focus on finding joy in simple things, such as a favorite song, a meal, or a fun moment with friends. At the end of the day, journal your thoughts.

Silver Dollar

Does your mind ever trap you in a story that you play out over and over? Did you know you can change the narrative? Think about a negative internal story you've been living out—for example, "I am anxious," "I am worthless," "I can't succeed." Try this meditation exercise to help let go of these narratives.

- Imagine a hole in the ground just large enough to put your hand in.

- Imagine you see a silver dollar at the bottom of the hole. It is stamped with the negative internal story you've chosen.

- Imagine you go to grab the silver dollar, but while you're grasping it, you discover your fist is now too big to fit back out of the hole.

- Clench your fist tightly, as if you're holding on to the silver dollar. Notice any sensations.

- Say to yourself, "I can release the coin and free my hand."

- Unclench your fist.

- Imagine hearing the coin drop back into the hole.

- Shake your hand.

- Say to yourself, "Holding on to that unpleasant story is not worth the dollar."

- Take four deep, slow breaths. Imagine removing your hand from the hole.

- Notice a sense of freedom after letting this story go.

What are you curious about in life? What inspires you to change? Write about something that makes you curious and how you could explore it further.

....

....

....

....

....

....

....

....

....

Do you pay attention to your heart? What does your heart long for or tell you today? Journal your thoughts.

DEALING
WITH DIFFICULTIES

When you have difficult or unpleasant feelings, how do you react? Do you try to ignore them? Do they overwhelm you? It can be challenging and confusing to deal with unpleasant feelings, but they don't have to rule you. Think of them like weather: always changing, not staying constant. When you can accept those feelings, in a sense, you're putting on a warm jacket to help you through life's stormy moments. This section of the journal will give you prompts and practices to help you remember that no feeling lasts forever and the storms will pass.

What is the story you have been told about anger? Is anger considered good or bad? How do you see anger demonstrated in your family? How do you choose to respond to anger?

In moments of anger or frustration, have some self-compassion—and extend that compassion to others. Try a positive affirmation like "May I have happiness and joy. May I be free from frustration and anger." Then turn it around: "May others have happiness and joy. May they be free from frustration and anger." What do you notice as you say this?

I'm Angry

Do you ever find yourself angry or frustrated about events or others' actions? If you can pause and realize you have a choice in how to respond, anger and frustration can dissipate. This exercise will show you how.

- Find a comfortable place to sit with your feet flat on the ground at a desk or table with this journal.

- Think about an incident that recently angered or frustrated you. Think about all the details. Once you start to feel the anger and frustration, write down specifically what angered or frustrated you:

. . . .

. . . .

. . . .

- Place one hand on your heart and one hand over your belly button.

- Say out loud, "I'm angry at ...." or "I'm frustrated with ...." Now say the same thing, but louder. Now say the same thing, but quieter.

- Notice any sensations in your body as you consider the incident. Notice any feelings and state them out loud (for example, "I feel hurt," "I feel sad," "I feel unimportant").

- Curl your toes and squeeze your hands. Then uncurl your toes and release your hands as you imagine releasing the anger and frustration. Repeat three times.

- Breathe in through your nose for a count of 5, hold your breath for a count of 7, breathe out through your mouth for a count of 8. Repeat three times.

- If there was another person involved in the incident, take a moment to consider what they may have been going through. Consider that they weren't trying to anger or frustrate you on purpose.

- Consider the statement "It's okay to feel these feelings. I can choose how I respond."

Write down four fears that get in your way. Then imagine rolling up this journal page and putting it in a bottle that you throw into the ocean. What would your life look like if you let those fears float away?

....

....

....

....

....

....

....

....

....

....

Do you tell yourself any sad stories? Maybe there has been something in the past week or month that caused some sadness. Were you comfortable with the sadness?

....

....

....

....

....

....

....

....

....

....

We've all experienced some emotional wounds. Acknowledging these wounds and releasing them can lead to healing. Draw a large heart below. Draw an open door in the center of the heart. Inside the door, write down anything that feels like an emotional wound. Imagine this door is letting these emotional wounds out so you can heal.

Do you ever wake up dreading the day ahead of you? It can help to develop a positive statement to handle the day, such as "This won't last forever." What are some positive statements that can help you get through a day you're dreading?

....

....

....

....

....

....

....

....

....

Consider a day you were dreading in the recent past. Did you have a thought like "This day will never end"? Write down what you dreaded. How did you get through the day? Did the feeling pass as the day went on?

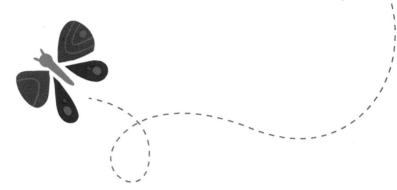

HEALING BEGINS
WHERE THE
WOUND WAS MADE.

—Alice Walker

Cradle

Mindfulness is being able to accept thoughts and feelings nonjudgmentally. Rather than push away difficult emotions, mindfulness can teach you to tolerate and sit with difficult feelings. Try this meditation to expand your ability to stay mindful and notice these difficult emotions.

- Find a comfortable place to sit.

- Breathe in deeply through your nose for a count of 5. Hold your breath for a count of 7. Breathe out through your mouth, forcefully, for a count of 8. Repeat four times.

- Think of a difficult experience from this past week. Consider for a moment the unpleasant feelings around that experience.

- Consider inviting the unpleasant emotions to move toward you.

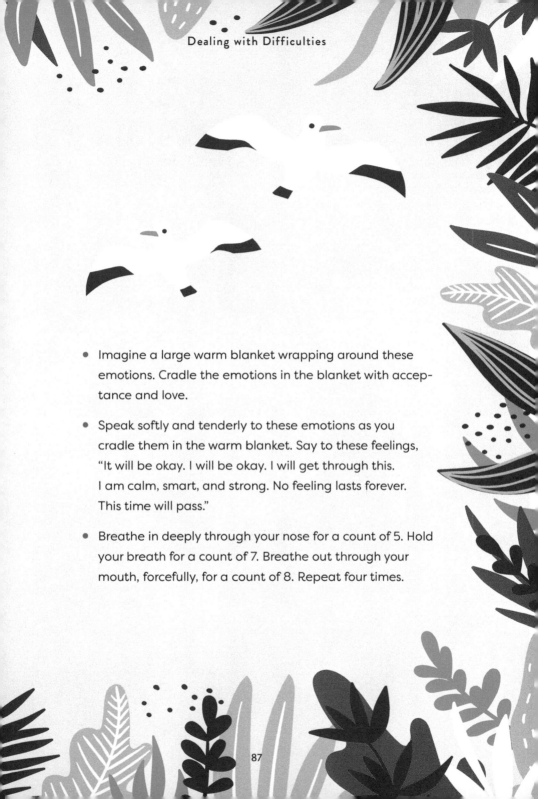

- Imagine a large warm blanket wrapping around these emotions. Cradle the emotions in the blanket with acceptance and love.

- Speak softly and tenderly to these emotions as you cradle them in the warm blanket. Say to these feelings, "It will be okay. I will be okay. I will get through this. I am calm, smart, and strong. No feeling lasts forever. This time will pass."

- Breathe in deeply through your nose for a count of 5. Hold your breath for a count of 7. Breathe out through your mouth, forcefully, for a count of 8. Repeat four times.

When I am experiencing emotional pain, the kindest
and most compassionate thing I can do for myself is . . .

Music can help shift a bad mood. Turn on a song and mindfully listen. Consider the lyrics, beat, and melody. Notice any physical sensations or feelings that arise as you listen. Notice any shift in your mood. Write about what you feel.

....

....

....

....

....

....

....

....

....

Emotional support from others can be helpful when you don't feel your best. Write a list of people you trust who can provide emotional support in your time of need. How do you feel when you think about them?

....

....

....

....

....

....

....

....

....

....

Do you ever feel like your days are filled with drama? Or catch yourself stirring up drama? What is one thing that happened today that was drama-free? What does it feel like when you're the subject of drama?

....

....

....

....

....

....

....

....

....

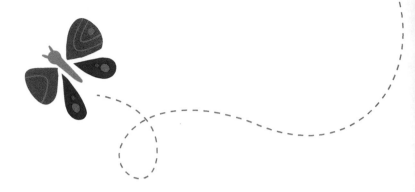

ON DAYS WHEN
THE SKY IS GRAY,
THE SUN HAS NOT
DISAPPEARED FOREVER.

—Arnaud Desjardins

When you notice unpleasant thoughts, it helps to ground yourself in the day and realize that thoughts are just thoughts. Try creating a personal mantra as follows: Today is [*day of the week*]. The date is [*date*]. I am at [*place*] (e.g., school, home). Although I am having thoughts or feelings of [*thought or feeling*], I can move through it. I am [*characteristic you like about yourself*] (e.g., strong, smart, competent).

A good cry can do wonders for your soul. Are you comfortable crying? Think about a recent time you cried or almost cried. Journal your thoughts.

....

....

....

....

....

....

....

....

....

....

Think about a time today you found yourself distracted or bored. Consider what you noticed and any bodily sensations you experienced. What can you do next time to help you stay mindful, not distracted?

The ABC Method

Have you ever needed to have a difficult conversation with a friend? The key to keeping your cool during a tough conversation is identifying the outcome you desire.

One way to do that is the ABC method:

- A is your feelings.
- B is the behavior or situation you experienced.
- C is your proposed solution.

Put it all together like this: "I felt A when I saw B happen, and I think it would make me feel better if you/we did C."

Now take a moment to think about a tough conversation you'd like to have a with a friend. Identify your feelings and what you need. Keeping mindful of what you need, look at yourself in a mirror and try the ABC method.

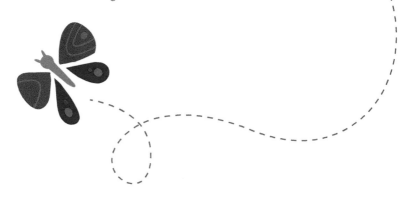

PAINFUL FEELINGS ARE,
BY THEIR VERY NATURE,
TEMPORARY . . .
THE ONLY WAY OUT
IS THROUGH.

—Kristin Neff

What would it be like to sit with uncomfortable feelings? What if you accepted that today you're angry or sad or annoyed, but tomorrow you could feel different?

....

....

....

....

....

....

....

....

....

....

On days when you want to just stay in bed, one way to get moving is to take a moment to be mindful of your daily tasks. Create a list of those tasks below and run through it one task at a time. Next time you feel depressed or unmotivated, say to yourself, "I can take care of one or two tasks," even if it's something small, like brushing your teeth. Often, once you start taking care of your task list, you'll feel a little better and be able to carry on with your day.

How do you receive feedback? Do you become defensive or take it as criticism, even when it comes from love, like "I'm concerned you're going to bed too late and feeling too tired the next day"? How might you see feedback as something to help you be a better you?

Jealousy comes from desiring something that isn't yours or a fear of losing something. Practicing compassion toward yourself can help you let go of jealousy. Write with compassion about a time you felt jealous. For example: "It's understandable I feel jealous that my friend got an A on that exam. Sometimes I worry my grades won't be good enough to get into the college of my choice. But I know I did my best and my grades don't define me."

A sincere apology includes three elements: accepting responsibility, not making excuses, and making amends. If you say, "I'm sorry, but . . . ," it's no longer an apology. Think of something you wish to apologize for and write a sincere apology.

....

....

....

....

....

....

....

....

....

Do you label difficult emotions as "bad" and try to run away from them? What if you took care of those emotions instead? Think of your heart as a nursery that can nurture "bad" emotions and show them love and kindness. Draw a small heart. Inside it, write an emotion you'd label as "bad" or "negative." Then draw a heart around that heart and another "bad" emotion inside that larger heart. Repeat until you run out of space. Say, "No feeling lasts forever. I can give myself some love when I don't feel so good."

LETTING IN THE LIGHT

Getting sucked into negativity or drama in life might feel familiar. When someone asks about your day, how often do you tell them about the bad but not the good? This section will help you find the joy and peace in your life by practicing compassion, being nonjudgmental toward yourself and others, and keeping your emotional responses under control. Practicing mindfulness and centering yourself in the present can let in the light of positive emotional states—and by now you may know that you can do that with breathing exercises, meditation, and journaling.

Think about some favorite moments from the past year. What made those moments great? What feelings did you experience?

....

....

....

....

....

....

....

....

....

....

....

When you're not having such a great day, what is
something kind you can do for yourself to help you get
through the day? Journal your thoughts.

I Hear You

Sometimes, instead of listening to what people are saying to us, we're already thinking about what we're going to say next. Here's how you can be a mindful listener using the HEAR technique.

- **Halt:** Put a halt to your thoughts and give your full attention to what the other person is saying.

- **Enjoy:** Take small breaths when someone talks to you. This will offer you a sense of calm before you speak.

- **Ask:** Did you understand what the other person was saying? If not, ask questions.

- **Reflect:** Start the conversation by repeating what they said so they know you were listening. Then give a nonjudgmental answer.

When you start a day with an intention such as "I will be patient today," it's like setting your GPS to arrive at your destination. What intentions do you want to live by today?

....

....

....

....

....

....

....

....

....

Try this: Envision achieving a goal you want to accomplish. Hold that image in your mind and take deep breaths. Send positive energy toward this goal. Think about small steps to take from now until your goal is met. Take four deep calming breaths before opening your eyes. Write down the action steps.

Inspiration helps spark creativity, confidence, and action. Think of people, places, or things that inspire you. Journal your thoughts.

Surprises can teach us something. For example, you may be dreading an event, but when you actually go, you're surprised to find you enjoy it. What has surprised you recently? Did it change your view on something?

Accept Yourself

Learning self-acceptance can sometimes take practice. This is a great exercise to help increase self-acceptance.

- Sit in a quiet corner and softly gaze at your hands in your lap.

- Take a deep breath in and then out. Keep doing this until you establish a rhythm.

- Bring all your feelings of not being accepted to the surface and let them go.

- Focus on yourself and one positive trait.

- Take a moment to extend self-love and compassion to yourself.

- Feel the air moving from your lungs and pay attention to the rise and fall of your abdomen.

- Open your eyes fully and mentally pat yourself on the back.

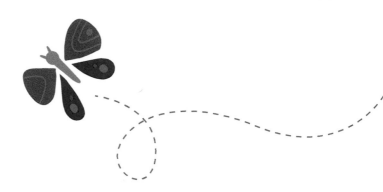

WHENEVER YOU LET GO OF SOMETHING NEGATIVE IN YOUR LIFE, YOU MAKE ROOM FOR SOMETHING POSITIVE.

—Cait Flanders

You! Who are you? Describe yourself with at least
10 words. What do you wish others knew about you?

Chocolate, kittens, reading, sleeping in on weekends . . . what brings you joy?

....

....

....

....

....

....

....

....

....

....

What are 10 things that make you smile? Write a list.

Consider your pleasant thoughts today. What feelings do you notice as you consider these thoughts? Journal about your pleasant thoughts and feelings.

Pick one area of your life in which to increase your mindfulness today, such as mindful eating or mindfully staying present in class. What are two or three ways to do that?

....

....

....

....

....

....

....

....

....

How are you feeling about the meditations in this journal so far? Have you been spending five minutes a day in meditation? Do you want to? Journal your thoughts about meditation.

Big Day

You can use mindfulness to help prepare for a test, sports event, or other challenge. Try this exercise when you wake up on the morning of the big day. It will help stop your mind from wandering and allow you to tap into your memory, so that you'll remember all the important information you need for the task ahead.

- Wake up early—the more you rush, the more stressed you'll be.

- Take a moment to stretch. Reach toward the ceiling and count to 10. Bend over, reach toward your toes, and count to 10. Repeat three times.

- Eat breakfast.

- Press your pinky finger and thumb together.

- Inhale for 4 seconds, hold your breath for 4 seconds, and exhale for 4 seconds.

- Focus your attention on three things: your chest rising, your breath going in and out, and the feeling of your fingers touching. Split your attention between these three. Welcome other thoughts and let them float away while bringing your focus back to your chest, breath, and fingers.

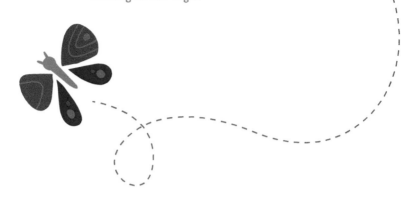

IF YOU WANT OTHERS TO BE HAPPY,

PRACTICE COMPASSION. IF YOU WANT TO BE HAPPY, PRACTICE COMPASSION.

—Dalai Lama

Let's answer the age-old question "What is love?" Take a moment to journal about love.

....

....

....

....

....

....

....

....

....

....

....

What qualities do you value in friendships? What makes you a good friend? Journal your thoughts.

....

....

....

....

....

....

....

....

....

....

A loving-kindness meditation is one of the cornerstone practices of mindfulness. This practice is simple yet powerful when practiced regularly.

- Find a comfortable place to sit.

- Say out loud or to yourself: "May I be at peace. May I be safe. May I be happy. May I have health. May others have peace. May others be safe. May others have happiness. May others have health." Repeat three times.

- Inhale deeply through your nose for a count of 5. Hold your breath for a count of 7. Exhale deeply through your mouth for a count of 8.

What feelings or sensations did you notice?

....

....

....

....

....

....

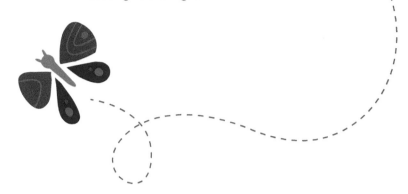

HAVE LOVE FOR YOUR INNER SELF, AND EVERYTHING ELSE IS DONE FOR YOU.

—Amit Ray

Healthy, Happy, Safe

Here's an exercise to help you focus on feelings of love.

- Find a quiet corner and sit down on a comfortable floor cushion or pillow. Close your eyes, take a few deep breaths, and imagine yourself standing in a circle surrounded by the people you love the most.

- Imagine all the attention, care, and energy you receive from these people. Repeat this message to yourself: "May I be healthy. May I be happy. May I be safe. Give me ease of heart."

- Let emotions rise and wash over you. Relish in the feeling of love that you're receiving from the circle and keep repeating the message like a mantra.

- Is your skin alive with energy? Love does that to you! You don't need to do anything special to deserve this kind of affection. Tell yourself you are loved simply because you exist.

- Now that you can feel the love coming toward you, send it back to others: "May we all be healthy. May we all be happy. May we all be safe. Give us ease of heart."

What are your strengths? Are you thoughtful, courageous, kind, persistent? How do your strengths help
you in your relationships and day-to-day activities?

....

....

....

....

....

....

....

....

....

How can you show yourself love? Positive self-talk, eating healthy foods, getting enough sleep? Write about ways you practice (and/or want to practice) self-love.

You've reached the end of the journal! Take a moment to reflect on your mindfulness journey so far. What were the biggest challenges? The biggest surprises? What mindfulness practices will you continue in the future?

....

....

....

....

....

....

....

....

....

RESOURCES

Apps

Stop, Breathe & Think App Quick five-minute exercises to help you extend compassion to yourself and stay in the present.

MindShift App Do you get caught in the anxiety trap? This app has some great exercises to help you tame that anxiety and feel freer and lighter throughout the day.

Smiling Mind App Who doesn't smile when they hear an Australian accent? Aside from the fun accent, the exercises are quick, easy, and impactful for helping you stay focused.

Take a Break App This app is for those moments when you say to yourself, "Wow, I need a break!" Use it as one of your go-to resources. You'll feel more relaxed and rejuvenated after you do.

Books

Mindfulness for Teens in 10 Minutes a Day: Exercises to Feel Calm, Stay Focused & Be Your Best Self by Jennie Marie Battistin, MA, LMFT

The Self-Compassion Workbook for Teens: Mindfulness and Compassion Skills to Overcome Self-Criticism and Embrace Who You Are by Karen Bluth, PhD

Get Out of Your Mind and Into Your Life for Teens: A Guide to Living an Extraordinary Life by Joseph V. Ciarrochi, PhD, Louise Hayes, PhD, and Ann Bailey, MA

Social Media

The Mindful Teen Facebook Group A great way to get a daily dose of inspirational thoughts to use in your mindfulness practice.

Mindful Hookup Instagram Page If you're feeling creative, @mindful_hookup is your ticket to learn how to make your own mindfulness journal, with beautiful examples of homemade bullet journal pages. Making journal pages can be a great mindfulness-based, stress-reducing exercise.

REFERENCES

Albertson, E. R., K. D. Neff, and K. E. Dill-Shackleford.
"Self-Compassion and Body Dissatisfaction in Women: A Randomized Controlled Trial of a Brief Meditation Intervention."
Mindfulness (2015) 6: 444. doi:10.1007/s12671-014-0277-3.

Ban Breathnach, Sarah. *Simple Abundance: A Daybook of Comfort and Joy.* New York: Grand Central Publishing, 2008.

Brach, Tara. *Radical Acceptance: Embracing Your Life with the Heart of a Buddha.* New York: Bantam, 2004.

Dalai Lama [Tenzin Gyatso] and Howard Cutler. *The Art of Happiness, 10th Anniversary Edition: A Handbook for Living.* New York: Riverhead Books, 2009.

Flanders, Cait. *The Year of Less: How I Stopped Shopping, Gave Away My Belongings, and Discovered Life is Worth More Than Anything You Can Buy in a Store.* New York: Hay House, 2018.

Hoge E. A., E. Bui, L. Marques, C. A. Metcalf, L. K. Morris, D. J. Robinaugh, J. J. Worthington, M. H. Pollack, N. M. Simon. "Randomized Controlled Trial of Mindfulness Meditation for Generalized Anxiety Disorder: Effects on Anxiety and Stress Reactivity." *Journal of Clinical Psychiatry* (August 2013) 8: 786–92. doi:10.4088/JCP.12m08083.

Kabat-Zinn, Jon. *Wherever You Go, There You Are: Mindfulness Meditation in Everyday Life.* New York: Hyperion, 1994.

Kapur, Shekhar. "We Are the Stories We Tell Ourselves." TEDIndia. November 2009. https://www.ted.com/talks/shekhar_kapur_we_are_the_stories_we_tell_ourselves/transcript?language=en.

Mock, Janet. *Redefining Realness: My Path to Womanhood, Identity, Love & So Much More.* New York: Atria, 2014.

Neff, Kristin. *Self-Compassion: The Proven Power of Being Kind to Yourself.* New York: William Morrow, 2012.

Nhất Hạnh, Thích. *The Miracle of Mindfulness.* New York: Beacon Press, 1999.

Ray, Amit. *Meditation: Insights and Inspirations.* Inner Light Publishers, 2010.

Rogers, Jodie. "The Stories We Tell Ourselves." TEDxBerklee Valencia. YouTube. Accessed August 21, 2019. www.youtube.com/watch?v=PXxBRhYseNY.

Walker, Alice. *The Way Forward Is with a Broken Heart*. New York: Ballantine Books, 2000.

Wolfelt, Alan D. *365 Meditations for Living in the Now*. Fort Collins, CO: Companion Press, 2017.

Zeidan, F.,S. K. Johnson, B. J. Diamond, Z. David, and P. Gool-kasian. "Mindfulness Meditation Improves Cognition: Evidence of Brief Mental Training." *Consciousness and Cognition* (June 2010) 2: 597–605. doi:10.1016/j.concog.2010.03.014

ABOUT THE AUTHOR

Jennie Marie Battistin, MA, LMFT, is a licensed marriage family therapist in the state of California. She graduated cum laude with a master's in clinical psychology from Pepperdine University in Malibu, California. Jennie Marie began her career working with teens on the Burbank High School campus. She has been a facilitator for *The Angst Movie: A Documentary on Anxiety*, which helped create a dialogue of support between students, teachers, and parents on the challenges of coping with anxiety. As a mother of five grown children, she has a strong passion for helping teens and parents develop tools and resources to help navigate challenges and mental health concerns facing today's teens. Jennie Marie is the founding director of Hope Therapy Center Inc. Marriage and Family Counseling of Burbank and Santa Clarita, with plans to expand offices to Orange County, California, and Washington State.

CPSIA information can be obtained
at www.ICGtesting.com
Printed in the USA
JSHW052138030121
10663JS00001B/2

9 781646 112838